FREEDOM
SUMMER, 1964

by Carla Mooney

Content Consultant
Keith Mayes, PhD
African American and African Studies
University of Minnesota

Core Library
An Imprint of Abdo Publishing
abdopublishing.com

abdopublishing.com

Published by Abdo Publishing, a division of ABDO, PO Box 398166, Minneapolis, Minnesota 55439. Copyright © 2016 by Abdo Consulting Group, Inc. International copyrights reserved in all countries. No part of this book may be reproduced in any form without written permission from the publisher. Core Library™ is a trademark and logo of Abdo Publishing.

Printed in the United States of America, North Mankato, Minnesota

042015
092015

Cover Photo: Horace Cort/AP Images
Interior Photos: Horace Cort/AP Images, 1; Bettmann/Corbis, 4, 17, 34, 39; Red Line Editorial, 8, 41; North Wind Picture Archives, 12, 15; Rogelio V. Solis/AP Images, 20; Eugene Smith/AP Images, 24; BH/AP Images, 27; AP Images, 30, 43; Gene Smith/AP Images, 36; Jack Thornell/AP Images, 45

Editor: Mirella Miller
Series Designer: Becky Daum

Library of Congress Control Number: 2015931579

Cataloging-in-Publication Data
Mooney, Carla.
 Freedom Summer, 1964 / Carla Mooney.
  p. cm. -- (Stories of the civil rights movement)
Includes bibliographical references and index.
ISBN 978-1-62403-878-5
1. African Americans--Civil rights--Mississippi--History--20th century--Juvenile literature. 2. African Americans--Suffrage--Mississippi--History--20th century--Juvenile literature. 3. Civil rights movements--Mississippi--History--20th century--Juvenile literature. 4. Civil rights workers--Mississippi--History--20th century--Juvenile literature.   I. Title.
323.1196--dc23
                                                              2015931579

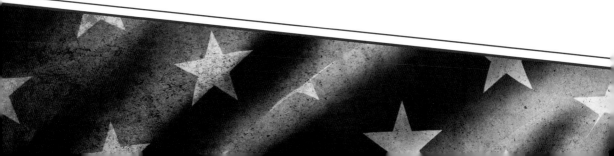

CONTENTS

MISSING CALL FBI

THE FBI IS SEEKING INFORMATION CONCERNING THE DISAPPEARANCE AT PHILADELPHIA, MISSISSIPPI, OF THESE THREE INDIVIDUALS ON JUNE 21, 1964. EXTENSIVE INVESTIGATION IS BEING CONDUCTED TO LOCATE GOODMAN, CHANEY, AND SCHWERNER, WHO ARE DESCRIBED AS FOLLOWS:

ANDREW GOODMAN	JAMES EARL CHANEY	MICHAEL HENRY SCHWERNER

	ANDREW GOODMAN	JAMES EARL CHANEY	MICHAEL HENRY SCHWERNER
RACE:	White	Negro	White
SEX:	Male	Male	Male
DOB:	November 23, 1943	May 30, 1943	November 6, 1939
POB:	New York City	Meridian, Mississippi	New York City
AGE:	20 years	21 years	24 years
HEIGHT:	5'10"	5'7"	5'9" to 5'10"
WEIGHT:	150 pounds	135 to 140 pounds	170 to 180 pounds
HAIR:	Dark brown; wavy	Black	Brown
EYES:	Brown	Brown	Light blue
TEETH:		Good: none missing	
SCARS AND MARKS:		1 inch cut scar 2 inches above left ear.	Pock mark center of forehead, slight scar on bridge of nose, appendectomy scar, broken leg scar.

SHOULD YOU HAVE OR IN THE FUTURE RECEIVE ANY INFORMATION CONCERNING THE WHEREABOUTS OF THESE INDIVIDUALS, YOU ARE REQUESTED TO NOTIFY ME OR THE NEAREST OFFICE OF THE FBI. TELEPHONE NUMBER IS LISTED BELOW.

Edgar Hoover

DIRECTOR
FEDERAL BUREAU OF INVESTIGATION
UNITED STATES DEPARTMENT OF JUSTICE
WASHINGTON, D. C. 20535
TELEPHONE, NATIONAL 8-7117

June 29, 1964

CHAPTER ONE

MISSING IN MISSISSIPPI

On the morning of June 21, 1964, three young men climbed into a station wagon in Meridian, Mississippi. Two were white men from the North. Michael Schwerner was from New York. He worked as a staff member for the Congress of Racial Equality (CORE), a civil rights group. Andrew Goodman was a volunteer college student from New York City. The third man, James Chaney, was a

Volunteers and activists of Freedom Summer knew their work could be dangerous.

Congress of Racial Equality

The Congress of Racial Equality (CORE) is a civil rights group. Founded in 1942, it had an important role in the civil rights movement. CORE was one of the main civil rights groups, of the 1960s along with the Southern Christian Leadership Conference, the Student Nonviolent Coordinating Committee (SNCC), and the National Association for the Advancement of Colored People (NAACP).

young African-American civil rights activist from Mississippi.

The three men were part of the 1964 Mississippi Summer Project, a nonviolent effort by civil rights activists to bring African Americans and whites together in Mississippi's segregated political system. The project would later be known as Freedom Summer. It was a grassroots movement. During the summer of 1964, hundreds of student volunteers from around the United States joined civil rights organizers and local African Americans in

Mississippi. At the time, Mississippi was one of the country's most racist and segregated states.

Together students and activists worked to stop Mississippi's whites from blocking African Americans from voting. They helped African Americans register to vote. They taught residents in special freedom schools. They provided legal and medical help at community centers. And they formed a new political party that was open to all people, the Mississippi Freedom Democratic Party (MFDP). They hoped to achieve equality and justice for all Americans.

The Ku Klux Klan, a white supremacy group, was very active in Mississippi. Klan members threatened to harm and kill African Americans and civil rights workers.

Arrested

On that morning of June 21, Schwerner, Goodman, and Chaney drove to Philadelphia, Mississippi. They visited Mount Zion Methodist Church. A few days earlier, Klan members had burned it down. As they

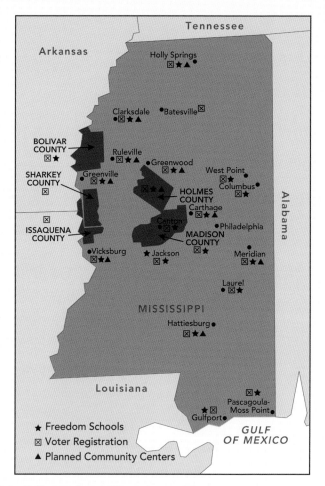

Mississippi Freedom Summer Map

The Mississippi Freedom Summer project involved hundreds of volunteers across Mississippi. The goals of the project included voter registration and education through freedom schools and community centers. This map shows the planned locations of several projects. Why do you think volunteers focused on these cities?

drove home, local police stopped the station wagon.

They arrested the three men. The police charged

Chaney with speeding, a violation often used by

the police to stop civil rights workers. They held Schwerner and Goodman for investigation. While in the Neshoba County Jail, the men were not allowed to call anyone.

Meanwhile, CORE staff members worried. The three men had not checked in. Later that night, the police released the men. They told them to leave Neshoba County. Schwerner, Goodman, and Chaney got into the station wagon. They were never seen alive again.

Missing

That night, word spread that the three men were missing. Local activists searched the woods for any trace of the men and their station wagon. Two days later, on June 23, a team of Federal Bureau of Investigation (FBI) investigators arrived.

Throughout the summer, investigators searched for the missing men. Six weeks into the search, investigators received a tip from a citizen. The tip led investigators to a dam on a farm in nearby

Philadelphia. On August 4, 1964, FBI agents found the bodies of the three men buried on the farm.

Capturing a Nation's Attention

The disappearance of Schwerner, Goodman, and Chaney was widely reported around the country. The disappearance and murder of the white and African-American activists brought the nation's attention to the racial violence in Mississippi.

People around the country were shocked at the violence in Mississippi. They were angry about the injustices African Americans living there faced. People asked the federal government to do something.

What Happened?

When the men were released from jail, the Neshoba County deputy sheriff called local Klan members. As the men drove down a rural road, the deputy sheriff and several Klan members stopped them. They shot and killed the men. They dumped their bodies at the farm and covered them with dirt. Then they burned the station wagon to destroy any evidence.

A Freedom Summer fact sheet was prepared at Stanford University and distributed to students interested in the project. This excerpt talks about the importance of white college students taking part in the movement:

> 3. . . . the moral support and concern of American students ignites a spark of hope in many communities, and ends the tremendous feeling of isolation or alienness and loneliness in their plight . . .
>
> 4. The white Northern student, inadvertently perhaps, gives additional strength to those native white Mississippians who recognize the need for social change, but who are still too timid to speak out in their 'closed society.'
>
> Source: "Information Sheet—Project Mississippi." Civil Rights Movement Veterans. Bruce Hartford, n.d. Web. Accessed February 9, 2015.

What's the Big Idea?

Take a close look at this fact sheet. What is its main idea? Pick out two details that support this idea. What can you tell about the recruitment process from this fact sheet?

CHAPTER TWO

MISSISSIPPI'S CLOSED SOCIETY

The United States has a long history of racial segregation. Starting in the 1600s, white colonists brought people from Africa to work as slaves. Slaves were the property of their owners. Slave owners could buy and sell slaves as they wished.

Opposing Slavery

Enslaved Africans were denied their most basic human rights. Many tried to escape by running away

Many slaves were forced to work on large plantations in the South.

from their slaveholders. Some white Americans also believed slavery was wrong. In the 1800s, these people tried to get the federal government to abolish slavery. Many people in the southern states did not support this. Their plantations and farms depended on slave labor. Southerners believed the federal government should not decide if slavery was legal. Instead they wanted each state to make its own decision.

The controversy over slavery was one of the reasons many southern states left the United States in 1860 and 1861. The disagreement between states led to the American Civil War (1861–1865). After the war, the states that had split rejoined the United States.

Constitutional Changes

In 1865 Congress passed the Thirteenth Amendment to the US Constitution. The Thirteenth Amendment abolished slavery throughout the United States. Congress then passed two more amendments that gave rights to the newly freed slaves. The Fourteenth

Citizens celebrated when the Fourteenth Amendment, protecting all citizens equally, was passed.

CIVIL RIGHTS VOICES
David Dennis

. . . it became clear that we had to do . . . something big. . . . Otherwise they'd simply continue to kill the best among us.

David Dennis was active in the civil rights movement in the 1960s. He served as the assistant director of the Council of Federated Organizations (COFO), an umbrella organization for the various civil rights groups in Mississippi. Dennis was also the leader of CORE's operations in Mississippi and Louisiana. He led CORE's efforts in the Freedom Summer project. An illness stopped Dennis from traveling with James Chaney, the young black man murdered along with two white volunteers during Freedom Summer.

Amendment made every person born in the United States a citizen. The Fifteenth Amendment gave African-American men the right to vote.

Racism and Jim Crow Laws

Many white southerners were angry that they were forced to end slavery. They did not see African Americans as equal citizens. They helped pass laws that made it hard for African Americans to be treated equally. These were called Jim Crow laws. Jim Crow laws segregated people based on race.

Jim Crow laws forced African Americans to use separate waiting rooms, schools, and bathrooms.

Jim Crow laws and segregation prevented most African Americans in Mississippi from voting or holding public office. In the 1950s, only 5 percent of African Americans in Mississippi were registered to vote. This was the lowest rate in the United States. Those who challenged Jim Crow laws faced danger. White supremacy groups killed, tortured, or beat them. White police officers disturbed and arrested them for made-up crimes. African Americans were also at risk of being fired from their jobs or kicked out of their homes. As a result, few African Americans in Mississippi registered to vote.

The organizers of Freedom Summer wanted to open Mississippi's closed society. They believed that getting African Americans involved in voting and politics was the key.

Ku Klux Klan

At the end of the Civil War, Confederate soldiers formed the Ku Klux Klan, a white supremacy group. The group opposed integration of the races. It worked to deny equal rights for African Americans. By the 1920s, the Klan boasted millions of members. In the 1950s and 1960s, the Klan used violence and threats to oppose the civil rights movement. They attacked and killed African Americans and sometimes whites who were trying to gain equal rights for African Americans in the South.

In the 1950s, 45 percent of Mississippi's residents were African American. By voting, they could have a voice in how their communities were being run.

EXPLORE ONLINE

The focus in Chapter Two is on the history of racism, segregation, and denying African Americans the right to vote in southern states. The website below also focuses on voter suppression in Mississippi. As you know, every source is different. How do the two sources present information differently? What can you learn from this website?

Background on Freedom Summer
mycorelibrary.com/freedom-summer

CHAPTER THREE

THE FREEDOM SUMMER PROJECT

Local civil rights activists had tried for years to get more African Americans registered to vote in Mississippi. White officials claimed that African Americans had little interest in voting. In 1963 several civil rights organizations set out to prove them wrong.

When Mississippi held an election for governor in November 1963, most African Americans were not able to vote in the election. To prove that African

Bob Moses was the director of Freedom Summer, and he recruited hundreds of student volunteers from northern colleges to participate in the project.

Americans wanted to vote, activists from several civil rights organizations created a mock election. They called it the Freedom Vote. Ninety-three thousand people cast ballots in the mock election. It showed the federal government and whites in Mississippi that African Americans wanted to vote.

Council of Federated Organizations

The Council of Federated Organizations (COFO) was a coalition of civil rights organizations working in Mississippi. It was established in 1962. Its goal was to maximize the efforts of the SNCC, CORE, and NAACP. COFO focused on voter registration and education. Led by SNCC activist Bob Moses, COFO launched the 1964 Mississippi Freedom Summer Project.

Making a Plan

After the success of the Freedom Vote, civil rights activist Bob Moses of the SNCC proposed a new plan. For ten weeks during the summer of 1964, white students from the North would join civil rights activists in Mississippi. Together they would work on a larger voter registration project.

Unlike the Freedom Vote, the new project would educate and register African Americans for real elections in 1964.

Organizers asked for white volunteers from northern colleges to join them. They hoped that the students would bring media attention to their cause. People would see the shocking violence and injustice in Mississippi. With increased attention, organizers believed that the federal government would be forced to step in.

In June 1964, student volunteers met at Western

CIVIL RIGHTS VOICES
Bob Moses

If it's possible this summer to have interracial teams living and working in Mississippi . . . communities, it might change the whole conception around the country of how it might be possible to get at some of these problems in the Deep South.

Bob Moses was a civil rights organizer from Harlem, New York. In 1960, Moses moved to Atlanta and began working with the SNCC. In 1964 Moses suggested the idea of Freedom Summer to the SNCC and COFO. He was also a key figure in the MFDP's challenge at the 1964 Democratic National Convention.

The majority of Freedom Summer volunteers remained determined to help African Americans in Mississippi after the men's disappearance.

College for Women in Oxford, Ohio. There they attended a weeklong orientation session. At the orientation, organizers warned the students that they would face opposition and danger in Mississippi.

On June 20, the first group of volunteers headed to Mississippi. The next day, the three civil rights workers, James Chaney, Michael Schwerner, and Andrew Goodman, were reported missing. The search for the missing men appeared in national headlines. It focused the nation's attention on Mississippi. As the days passed, people began to fear the worst. They believed that the Klan had murdered the men.

No Turning Back

Freedom Summer volunteers did not turn back after the men's disappearance. The volunteers spread throughout the state. Nearly 1,500 volunteers worked in project offices across Mississippi. Students, clergy, attorneys, and medical professionals worked with civil rights activists. Many stayed with local African-American families.

Registering Voters

Voter registration was one of the project's main goals. Volunteers and civil rights activists worked to register African-American voters. They wanted to convince as many people as possible to join the voting process.

Approximately 17,000 African Americans attempted to register to vote in the summer of 1964. However, local registrars accepted only 1,600 applications. They claimed the African-American applicants did not pass the state-required literacy test. Those who tried to register braved harassment, threats, and violence. The harassment and injuries they faced made the national news. Public outrage grew. Many urged the federal government to get involved. They called for federal voting rights legislation.

Freedom Schools and Community Centers

In early July, volunteers opened the first freedom schools in Mississippi. African-American schools in Mississippi were separate and unequal. Volunteers hoped to address this inequality through freedom schools. African Americans of all ages came for classes on traditional subjects such as math and reading. They also learned about African-American history, the civil rights movement, citizenship, and leadership skills.

More than 2,000 students enrolled in classes at freedom schools led by approximately 175 teachers.

Volunteer teachers hoped these classes would give African Americans the tools they needed to carry on fighting against injustice after the summer volunteers had returned home. By the end of Freedom Summer, there were more than 40 freedom schools in 20 communities.

Volunteers also opened community centers. They provided legal and medical aid to residents. They offered childcare, library books, meals, and other services normally denied to African Americans.

Opposition

Several white groups in Mississippi opposed the Freedom Summer project. The state's senators and governor refused to obey federal laws to allow the races to mix. Legislators passed laws to forbid some protests and the passing out of informational brochures. Local sheriffs and police departments increased their forces and bought new weapons.

Many business leaders in Mississippi also opposed the efforts to include African Americans in the voting process. Some people banned African-American customers from stores.

In many cases, the opposition turned violent. The Klan harassed and threatened African-American residents and civil rights workers. Between June 16 and September 30, 1964, there were murders, shootings, bombings, beatings, and arrests of civil rights workers and local residents.

Freedom Summer volunteer Terri Shaw traveled to Mississippi to work at the COFO office in Hattiesburg. In this account, she describes the violence volunteers faced:

> . . . most serious incidents concerning volunteers were beatings. The first occurred on July 10 when the Rabbi Arthur Lelyveld of Cleveland . . . and two white male college students were beaten while on their way to one of the churches. . . . They were attacked by two white men who had been following them in a pickup truck without license plates . . . they beat the rabbi and one of the students with an iron bar. The other student was kicked down an embankment, pummeled and kicked . . .
>
> White people watched the beating from their porches and front lawns, but no one called the police until other volunteers returned to the scene to look for the rabbi's glasses.

> Source: Terri Shaw. "One Volunteer's Freedom Summer, 1964." American Experience. WGBH Educational Foundation, August 23, 2006. Web. Accessed February 9, 2015.

Back It Up

Terri Shaw is using evidence to support a point. Write a paragraph describing the point Shaw is making. Include two or three pieces of evidence she uses to make the point.

CHAPTER FOUR

CHALLENGING THE POLITICAL SYSTEM

I n early 1964, organizers of Freedom Summer created a new political party. They named it the Mississippi Freedom Democratic Party (MFDP). Though the MFDP was created and led by African Americans, it was open to all people, regardless of race.

The Mississippi Freedom Democratic Party called for delegates from their party to represent Mississippi at the Democratic National Convention in 1964.

Student Nonviolent Coordinating Committee

The Student Nonviolent Coordinating Committee (SNCC) was one of the most important groups of the civil rights movement. The SNCC was originally created to organize and tell people about student sit-in protests. Over the years, the SNCC grew to become a large organization. Many northern supporters raised money to fund the SNCC's work in the South. The SNCC had a key role in many important moments of the civil rights movement, including the 1961 Freedom Rides, the 1963 March on Washington, Mississippi Freedom Summer, and the MFDP.

Challenged

In August 1964, the MFDP challenged Mississippi's Democratic Party at the Democratic National Convention. It was a presidential election year. Mississippi's Democratic Party planned to send a group of all-white delegates to the convention. The MFDP protested.

With the help of Freedom Summer volunteers and the SNCC, activists gathered the signatures of thousands of African Americans. The MFDP held its own state convention in early August and elected delegates.

At the convention, the MFDP asked officials to recognize their delegation instead of the all-white delegation. They argued that, because African-American residents had not been allowed to select the all-white delegation, it should not represent the state. MFDP delegate Fannie Lou Hamer spoke to the Democratic Party's credentials committee in a nationally televised speech. The convention still refused to seat MFDP delegates.

CIVIL RIGHTS VOICES
Fannie Lou Hamer

Is this America, the land of the free and the home of the brave, where we have to sleep with our telephones off of the hooks because our lives be threatened daily, because we want to live as decent human beings, in America? Fannie Lou Hamer dedicated her life to the fight for civil rights. She had been beaten while trying to register to vote. Hamer worked for the SNCC to fight racial segregation and injustice in the South. In 1964, she helped found the Mississippi Freedom Democratic Party.

Although the MFDP failed to gain seats at the DNC or in Congress, it was ultimately successful in bringing attention to voting injustices.

Freedom Election

In November registered voters across the nation voted for a presidential candidate and for people to fill local offices. Many African Americans in Mississippi had tried to register to vote, but they were denied. Instead Freedom Summer leaders held a Freedom Election from October 31 to November 2.

More than 68,000 people cast votes. In most counties, Freedom voters numbered more than regular Democratic Party voters. The election turnout proved that African Americans would vote in large numbers if they were given the opportunity.

In the regular November election, the Mississippi Democratic Party elected white representatives to Congress. The MFDP argued that this was not valid because they had not been elected by a majority of the state's voters. The US House of Representatives eventually denied the MFDP challenge. They seated the white election winners. But the struggle of MFDP leaders brought the nation's attention to voting rights in Mississippi.

FURTHER EVIDENCE

There is quite a bit of information about the MFDP in Chapter Four. What is one of the chapter's main points? What evidence is included to support this point? Read the article at the website below. Find a quote from the website that supports the chapter's main point.

MFDP Challenge to the Democratic Convention

mycorelibrary.com/freedom-summer

CHAPTER FIVE

THE IMPACT OF FREEDOM SUMMER

With the help of Freedom Summer volunteers, thousands of African Americans in Mississippi stepped forward to claim their right to vote during the summer of 1964. They braved violence and intimidation. News coverage of Freedom Summer opened the eyes of many Americans. People from New York to California were angered by the events in Mississippi and the denial of rights

Freedom Summer volunteers work together on a training program for African-American voter registration.

to African-American citizens. The killing of civil rights workers shocked them. Millions of Americans recognized the need for change.

The impact of Freedom Summer continued long after the volunteers left Mississippi. Many Freedom Summer projects continued and new programs started to help African Americans in the South. President Lyndon B. Johnson's administration gave funding for health clinics and school programs. Project Head Start, a national preschool program, emerged from Freedom Summer. Other nutrition and legal aid programs also continued to help African-American residents.

Disillusioned

By the fall of 1964, many Freedom Summer organizers were discouraged. The brutal response of the white opposition convinced some that nonviolent efforts could not succeed. Others were unhappy with the federal government's refusal to get involved and enforce civil rights laws. Some activists, such as Malcolm X, believed that African Americans needed to be more forceful and demand their basic civil rights.

Freedom Summer led to significant changes in the United States, such as the Civil Rights Act of 1964.

New Legislation

In July 1964, Congress passed the Civil Rights Act of 1964. It gave equal rights to all people, no matter their race, color, religion, gender, or national origin.

The next year, Congress passed the Voting Rights Act of 1965. The act made it illegal to discriminate against people who wanted to register to vote because of their race. It allowed the federal government to send its own officials to local

Punishment for Freedom Summer Murders

Eventually federal prosecutors convicted seven men of civil rights violations related to the murders of Michael Schwerner, Andrew Goodman, and James Chaney. Several others were found not guilty. None were convicted of murder. Edgar Ray Killen was acquitted because a member of the jury did not want to convict a preacher. Many years later, some of the men involved admitted that Killen had planned the murders. In 2004 the Mississippi State Attorney General announced that he was gathering evidence to charge Killen with murder. In 2005 Killen was found guilty of manslaughter. He was sentenced to 60 years in prison.

courthouses in order to enforce the new law. The act has helped millions of African Americans exercise their right to vote. It opened doors for diverse candidates to be elected to all levels of government.

Opening a Nation's Eyes

The brave volunteers and participants in the Freedom Summer project opened the nation's eyes to the civil rights injustices in the South. Although the struggle against racism was not over in the United States, denying a citizen

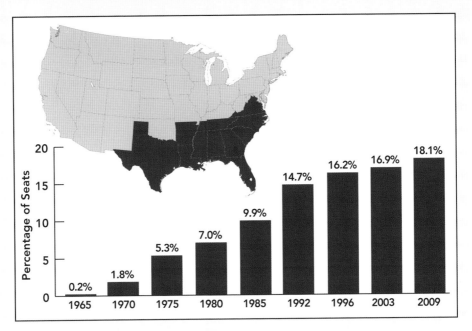

The Fight for Voting Rights

Since the passage of the Voting Rights Act of 1965, African Americans have steadily gained seats in the legislatures of several southern states. After reading this book, how do you think the work of Freedom Summer volunteers and the civil rights movement impacted these numbers?

the right to vote based on his or her race was now against the law.

By the end of 1966, more than half of African Americans in the South had registered to vote. In later years, many were elected to local and statewide offices.

SNAPSHOT OF FREEDOM SUMMER

Michael Schwerner, Andrew Goodman, and James Chaney were three Freedom Summer volunteers who were murdered in the summer of 1964. The murders burned the men's station wagon to try to destroy the evidence. These men, along with a number of other white and African-American volunteers, worked together across Mississippi on voter registration and other Freedom Summer projects.

Date
Summer 1964

Key Players
Civil rights activists Bob Moses and David Dennis, hundreds of student volunteers including Michael Schwerner, Andrew Goodman, and James Chaney.

What Happened

In 1964, white students worked alongside African-American civil rights activists in a grassroots effort to expand voter registration in Mississippi. They also worked to educate African Americans in freedom schools and community centers. At the time, Mississippi was one of the country's most segregated and racist states.

Impact

The events of Freedom Summer focused the nation's attention on the crisis in Mississippi and the barriers that African Americans faced.

STOP AND THINK

Say What?

Studying the civil rights movement can mean learning a lot of new vocabulary. Find five words in this book that you've never seen or heard before. Use a dictionary to find out what they mean. Then write the meanings in your own words, and use each word in a new sentence.

Why Do I Care?

You did not grow up during the civil rights movement. But that doesn't mean it hasn't affected your life. Think about two or three ways the struggles and actions of the Freedom Summer connect to your own life. Give examples of parts of your life that have a connection to Freedom Summer.

Tell the Tale

This book discusses Freedom Summer and the struggle for the right to vote. Imagine you lived during the civil rights movement. Write 200 words about life during this time. What events do you see taking place? What is happening in the news each day?

Dig Deeper

After reading this book, what questions do you still have about Freedom Summer? With an adult's help, find a few reliable sources that can help you answer your questions. Write a paragraph about what you learned.

GLOSSARY

abolish
to formally put an end to a practice, such as slavery

manslaughter
intentional killing of a human being, without planning in advance

activists
people who campaign for social change

opposition
the action of resisting

delegates
people sent or authorized to represent others

segregated
people separated according to race, sexual orientation, gender, or religious beliefs

injustices
things that lack justice or fairness

suppression
the act of not allowing something to happen such as an activity or publication

LEARN MORE

Books

Edmonds, Michael. *Risking Everything: A Freedom Summer Reader.* Madison: Wisconsin Historical Society Press, 2014.

Mitchell, Don. *The Freedom Summer Murders.* New York: Scholastic Press, 2014.

Rubin, Susan Goldman. *Freedom Summer: The 1964 Struggle for Civil Rights in Mississippi.* New York: Holiday House, 2014.

Websites

To learn more about Stories of the Civil Rights Movement, visit **booklinks.abdopublishing.com**. These links are routinely monitored and updated to provide the most current information available.

Visit **mycorelibrary.com** for free additional tools for teachers and students.

INDEX

ABOUT THE AUTHOR

Carla Mooney is the author of several books for young readers. A graduate of the University of Pennsylvania, she lives in Pittsburgh, Pennsylvania, with her husband and three children.